12/06

Robert Goddard

by Lola M. Schaefer

Consulting Editor: Gail Saunders-Smith, Ph.D.
Consultant: James Gerard, Aerospace Education
Specialist, Kennedy Space Center

Pebble Books

an imprint of Capstone Press
Mankato, Minnesota

Pebble Books are published by Capstone Press
151 Good Counsel Drive, P.O. Box 669, Mankato, Minnesota 56002
http://www.capstone-press.com

1 2 3 4 5 6 05 04 03 02 01 00

Library of Congress Cataloging-in-Publication Data
Schaefer, Lola M., 1950–
    Robert Goddard/by Lola M. Schaefer.
    p. cm.—(Famous people in transportation)
    Includes bibliographical references and index.
    Summary: Simple text and photographs present the life of the scientist who
developed the first liquid propelled rocket.
    ISBN 0-7368-0548-6
    1. Goddard, Robert Hutchings, 1882–1945—Juvenile literature. 2. Rocketry—
United States—Biography—Juvenile literature. [1. Goddard, Robert Hutchings,
1882–1945. 2. Scientists. 3. Rocketry—Biography.] I. Title. II. Series.
TL781.85.G6 S33   2000
629.4'092—dc21
[B]   99-047363

Note to Parents and Teachers

The series Famous People in Transportation supports national social studies standards related to the ways technology has changed people's lives. This book describes the life of Robert Goddard and illustrates his contributions to transportation. The photographs support early readers in understanding the text. This book also introduces early readers to subject-specific vocabulary words, which are defined in the Words to Know section. Early readers may need assistance to read some words and to use the Table of Contents, Words to Know, Read More, Internet Sites, and Index/Word List sections of the book.

Table of Contents

4

Robert Goddard was born in Massachusetts in 1882. He grew up on a farm. He wondered how machines and other things worked.

6

Robert read science fiction stories about people flying into space. Robert wondered if space travel might be possible someday.

of balloon; 20 miles
limit of atmosphere
200 miles
700 miles
6 miles/s
1 lb

Robert studied science for many years. He became a college teacher in 1911. He also experimented with rockets. Robert tested different rocket shapes and fuels.

10

Robert met Esther Fisk.
Robert and Esther married
in 1924. She believed in
Robert's rocket work.

11

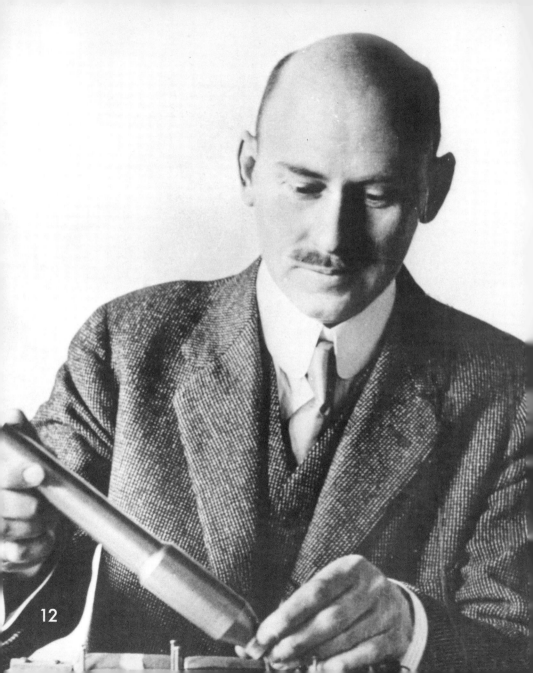

Solid fuel powered small rockets until the early 1900s. Robert made a liquid fuel with liquid oxygen and gasoline. This fuel made rockets more powerful.

14

Robert launched the first liquid-fuel rocket in 1926. The rocket traveled 60 miles (97 kilometers) per hour. It traveled 41 feet (12 meters) into the air.

16

Robert worked hard for many years. He made rockets that were bigger and more powerful. He tested many rockets. Some rockets worked. Some rockets did not work.

Robert wanted his rockets to be useful. He began to help the U.S. Navy build rockets in 1942.

WHO IS
DR. GODDARD?

HOW DO
WE [TAKE?]
SP

20

Robert Goddard died in 1945. The government named a space flight center after Robert in 1959. Rocket scientists still use many of Robert's ideas today.

Words to Know

experiment—to plan to try something new

fuel—a source of energy; early rockets used solid fuels such as gunpowder; Robert Goddard made the first liquid-fuel rocket.

gasoline—a liquid fuel made from oil

launch—to send off; rockets use a lot of fuel when they are launched.

oxygen—an element that usually is a colorless gas; oxygen turns into a liquid when it is very cold; liquid oxygen helps fuels burn.

rocket—a vehicle usually shaped like a long tube with a pointed end; rockets move by pushing fuel from one end.

science—the study of the natural and physical world; astronomy, biology, geology, and physics are sciences.

science fiction—stories that tell about the way real or pretend science can change people and the world; science fiction stories may be about life in the future or life on other planets.

Read More

Maurer, Richard. *Rocket!: How a Toy Launched the Space Age.* New York: Crown Publishers, 1995.

Streissguth, Thomas. *Rocket Man: The Story of Robert Goddard.* Minneapolis: Carolrhoda, 1995.

Vogt, Gregory L. *Rockets.* Explore Space! Mankato, Minn.: Bridgestone Books, 1999.

Internet Sites

Build-a-Rocket
http://www.rahul.net/renoir/rocket

The First Liquid Fuel Rocket
http://pao.gsfc.nasa.gov/gsfc/service/gallery/
fact_sheets/general/frocket/frocket.htm

Principles of Aeronautics
http://wings.ucdavis.edu/Book/beginner.html

Robert H. Goddard: American Rocket Pioneer
http://pao.gsfc.nasa.gov/gsfc/service/gallery/
fact_sheets/general/goddard/goddard.htm

Index/Word List

college, 9
experimented, 9
farm, 5
Fisk, Esther, 11
fuel, 9, 13
gasoline, 13
government, 21
ideas, 21
liquid oxygen, 13
machines, 5
Massachusetts, 5

rocket, 9, 11, 13, 15, 17, 19, 21
science, 9
science fiction, 7
scientists, 21
space, 7
space flight center, 21
teacher, 9
tested, 9, 17
travel, 7
U.S. Navy, 19

Word Count: 203
Early-Intervention Level: 17

Editorial Credits
Martha E. H. Rustad, editor; Kia Bielke, cover designer; Kimberly Danger, photo researcher

Photo Credits
Archive, 6
NASA, cover inset, 1, 4, 8, 10, 12, 14, 16, 18
Uniphoto/Ron Solomon, 20
UPI/Corbis-Bettmann, cover